Savannah S

A Keepsake Tour of Gardens, Architecture, and Monuments

Robert J. Hill, II

Schiffer
Publishing Ltd

4880 Lower Valley Road, Atglen, PA 19310 USA

Dedication

I dedicate this book in honor of Amber, my angel and my muse, and in memory of Doodle and Schmee, two little people with fur and fangs who left us in Savannah. With special thanks to my parents, Clara and Gary, and my brother, Mark, for making our first Savannah visits so much fun.

Find more Savannah information online at www.SavannahSquares.com.

Copyright © 2004 by Robert J. Hill, II
Library of Congress Card Number: 2004103708

Cover Photo: Orleans Square
Designed by John P. Cheek
Type set in Korinna BT

ISBN: 0-7643-2047-5
Printed in China

Published by Schiffer Publishing Ltd.
4880 Lower Valley Road
Atglen, PA 19310
Phone: (610) 593-1777; Fax: (610) 593-2002
E-mail: Info@schifferbooks.com

For the largest selection of fine reference books on this and related subjects, please visit our web site at **www.schifferbooks.com**
We are always looking for people to write books on new and related subjects. If you have an idea for a book please contact us at the above address.

This book may be purchased from the publisher.
Include $3.95 for shipping.
Please try your bookstore first.
You may write for a free catalog.

In Europe, Schiffer books are distributed by
Bushwood Books
6 Marksbury Ave.
Kew Gardens
Surrey TW9 4JF England
Phone: 44 (0) 20 8392-8585; Fax: 44 (0) 20 8392-9876
E-mail: info@bushwoodbooks.co.uk
Free postage in the U.K., Europe; air mail at cost.

Contents

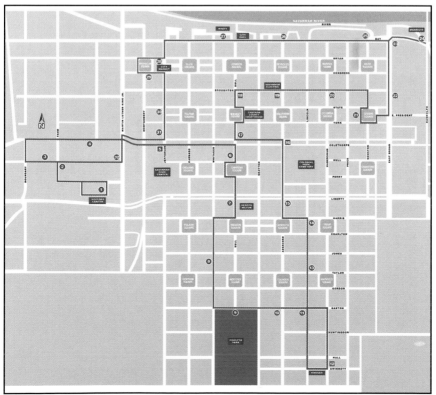

Foreword

How did you discover the charm and beauty of Savannah? Maybe you chuckled when you first heard or read about the "Savannah Way" of doing things? Or maybe your eyes went wide open when bright pink azaleas burst from Spanish moss shadows on a movie screen? Or maybe, if you were really lucky, you discovered the charm and beauty of Savannah in person.

I was really lucky because I discovered Savannah in person, as a child on summer vacation with my parents. Savannah, with nearby Tybee Island and Forts Pulaski, Jackson, and McAlister, offered my family everything: adventure, art, architecture, gardens, ghost stories, and plain old-fashioned history.

Today, I live in Savannah and I still enjoy adventure, art, architecture, gardens, and ghost stories, but her history fascinates me most. For that reason, I am drawn to Savannah's twenty-three public squares. As I look in and around her squares, I see their beautiful azaleas, expansive live oaks, and draping Spanish moss beside so many romantically and tragically storied homes and gardens. As I view the monuments, memorials, fountains, and plaques, I learn about the people and events that created Savannah. As I stand in the squares, I understand that the history of the squares is, in fact, the history of Savannah.

I hope that you use this book to discover Savannah in person. That "the Savannah Way" of doing things amuses you. That the "What'll ya drink?" party-side of Savannah thrills you. And that the beauty of pink color-dripping azaleas, the shade of expansive live oaks, and the gray whisps of draping Spanish moss draw you back to Savannah again and again.

Robert Hill
Savannah, Georgia
May 2003

A Brief History of Savannah

Shady gray Spanish moss drapes down long-limbed live oaks. Azaleas bushy bloom and burst in pretty pink shades all around. Savannah springs in eye-catching color and seduces in subtle shadows of green and gray everywhere—but especially in her squares. Savannah has America's largest historic district and within it she holds twenty-three public squares. Savannah's squares have long-served her as everything from outdoor meeting halls to musical parlors. Savannah was actually created around her squares by the very people and events she now commemorates in her squares. As a result, the history of her squares is very much the history of Savannah.

Savannah has always been rather "eccentric." In 1733, General James Oglethorpe founded Savannah as the first city in the British colony of Georgia. Unlike other British colonies, Georgia was established and governed for its first twenty years as a private Trust colony—not as a Crown colony. The Trust had three goals for Georgia. First, the Trust wanted to give "worthy but unfortunate" Britons a fresh start at "farming self-sufficiency." Second, the Trust wanted to make Georgia a self-sufficient raw materials supplier for British goods manufacturers. Finally, the Trust wanted Georgia to protect the well-established and profitable British Carolinas from Spanish Florida.

Savannah was the capitol of what other colonials called "The Odd Colony" because the Trust took odd measures to attain its three goals for Georgia. First, the Trust prohibited the production and sale of liquor in Georgia. Thirsty Georgians were lucky, though, that liquor was produced and sold freely in the Carolinas. Second, the Trust leased but did not sell Georgia lands to Georgians. As a result, most Georgians had no pride in land ownership and failed to care for leased lands. The altruistic Trust also prohibited slavery. Unfortunately, without slave labor Georgians could not grow profitable but labor-intensive crops like cotton. In 1754, the Trust gave up colonial management and Georgia became a Crown colony.

Savannah was America's second planned city (Philadelphia, Pennsylvania, was first). When Oglethorpe landed on the banks of Savannah River and negotiated with Yamacraw Indian Chief Tomochichi for land, he had a plan for "Savannah Towne." Experts speculate that Oglethorpe based Savannah's easily repeatable system of self-sufficient wards on English, Roman, or Chinese designs. Whatever the inspiration, each ward had forty building lots, four trust lots, and a square at its center. Each building lot was assigned one five-acre garden lot inside the town boundaries and one forty-five-acre farm lot outside the town boundaries. The trust lots were used by churches, school, and other public service providers. The squares were used as common meeting areas, stockyards, and for refuge from Indian attacks. Before he permanently returned to Britain in 1742, Oglethorpe personally oversaw the development of Savannah' six pre-Revolutionary squares.

Savannah now attracts millions of vistors annually, but for most of her years, few people stayed long in Savannah. Only one colonist (Noble Jones, founder of Wormsloe Plantation) arrived with Oglethorpe in 1733 and survived to see the crown assume control over Georgia in 1754. Too often, Savannah was just plain inhospitable. Untold numbers of Savannahians died during colonial "wars" with Spanish Florida, the Revolutionary War-era Siege of Savannah, the War of 1812, and the Civil War. Countless numbers of Savannahians died during yellow fever epidemics, lowland flooding, catastrophic fires, and other "natural" disasters. Savannah was its own economic disaster until legalized slavery made rice production profitable. Then, after the Revolutionary War and after Eli Whitney invented the cotton gin at nearby Mulberry Grove Plantation, Savannah began to thrive, not as a cotton producer, but as a cotton shipping port.

Savannah largely owes its wealth and its melting pot background to its location and its development as a major international shipping port. When the Central of Georgia Railroad eased trade between Savannah and inland cotton plantations, Savannah boomed! Savannah experienced its "Golden Age" between the American Revolution and the Civil War, while cotton was "king." During its Golden Age, Savannah added wards with many fine mansions before she physically capped the development of future Oglethorpe-styled wards with Forsyth Park. Today Savannah is America's fifth busiest shipping port but much of her good fortune comes from leisure visitors.

Today, the "Hostess City of the South" welcomes one and all with a new face. Sherman did not burn her, but he burned the plantations that sent Savannah her lifeblood cotton. After the Civil War, cotton production prices increased and Savannah nearly starved to death, literally. Over the next century, Savannah expanded into suburbs and largely neglected her historic heart. Then, in the 1950s, businesses and people started returning to the historic district. With three squares damaged and several historic buildings threatened, several concerned ladies of Savannah formed the Historic Savannah Foundation to protect and renovate the historic district. Over the last fifty years, the Foundation, innumerable private real estate investors, and the city of Savannah have preserved hundreds of Savannah's historic buildings and completely renovated each of the squares. Savannah is now experiencing her second "Golden Age" and countless books, movies, and travelers bear witness: Savannah subtly seduces and beautifully bedazzles!

The historical information in this book was compiled from state and civic historical markers, monuments and plaque inscriptions and from these other excellent sources:

City of Savannah, City of Savannah Online, www.ci.savannah.ga.us (12 June 2003.)

Savannah Convention and Visitors Bureau, Savannah Convention and Visitors Bureau Online, www.savcvb.com (12 June 2003).

Savannah Now, Savannah Morning News on the Web, http://Savannahnow.com/stories/070603/OPEDopedports.shtml (6 July 2003)

Sieg, Edward Chan. *The Squares: An Introduction to Savannah*. Virginia Beach, Virginia: The Donning Company, 1984.

Toledano, Roulhac. *The National Trust Guide to Savannah: Architectural & Cultural Treasures*. Hoboken, New Jersey: John Wiley & Sons, Inc., 1997.

A Guide to Using This Book

This book was organized in chronological, and somewhat geographical, order. As the text reveals, Savannah was created around her squares in successive order from Johnson, the first one on the river, through Whitefield, the last and one of the farthest from the river.

Savannah visitors typically begin walking tours in the older squares nearest the river and proceed out toward Monterey (made famous in *Midnight in the Garden of Good and Evil*) and the last line of squares lying farthest from the river. I have taken many tours of Savannah and all of them proceeded in the same geographical order.

By visiting the squares in chronological order, you can understand why the history of the squares is, in fact, the history of Savannah.

Johnson Square

Johnson Square (1733) is named for the Royal Governor of South Carolina who protected Georgia's first colonists. In 1733, the first church service and the first colonial Georgian birth—of a girl named Georgia Close—both occurred near this square. In 1819, a presidential reception in this square preceded the launch of the historic U.S.S. Savannah steamship. In 1825, the Marquis de Lafayette dedicated the obelisk in the center of this square (pictured) for General Nathanael Greene who—in 1901—was exhumed from Colonial Park Cemetery and re-interred under the obelisk. The sundial on the southern side of this square honors Colonel William Bull who first surveyed Savannah. Note that Savannah dyes the water green in many of her fountains (pictured) just before St. Patrick's Day every year.

Near this square: Christ Episcopal Church (1897) at 28 Bull Street is "Georgia's Mother Church" because a church building has occupied the lot since Oglethorpe's day. The Reverend John Wesley started America's "Sunday School" tradition while rector of this church. The Savannah Bank Building (1911) at 2-6 East Bryan Street was Savannah's first "skyscraper." The First Union Building across this square is now Savannah's tallest building.

Telfair Square

Telfair Square (1733) is now named for merchant and three-time Georgia Governor Edward Telfair and his philanthropic daughters, Margaret and Mary. Originally, this square was named after St. James Square in London and many mansions were built beside it. In fact, the Telfair Museum of Art (once the Telfair family mansion) now stands where the Royal Governor's Mansion once stood. Trinity Methodist Church, stands where the Telfair family gardens and the Sheftall House once stood.

Near this square: The Telfair Museum of Art (1818) at 121 Barnard Street occupies the Telfair family mansion designed by noted American architect William Jay. Statues of Phidias, Raphael, Rubens, Michelangelo, and Rembrandt now stand in front of "the Telfair," one of the oldest museums in the South. Trinity United Methodist Church (1848) on Barnard Street is Savannah's oldest Methodist Church.

Oglethorpe Square

Oglethorpe Square (1734) is now named for Georgia founder General James Oglethorpe, but originally it was named Upper New Square. In the northeast corner of this square, a marker honors America's first Moravian colonists. The Moravians were musicians and religious pacifists who started a school for Indians in the nearby community of Irene in 1736. Unfortunately, when war erupted between England and Spain in 1740, the Moravians sold their musical instruments to finance their relocation to Philadelphia.

Near this square: The Richard-Owens-Thomas House (1819, pictured) at 124 Abercorn Street was designed by noted American architect William Jay, and is now owned by the Telfair Museum of Art. The US Customs House (1852) at 1-5 East Bay Street housed the infamous Wanderer slave ship trial in 1859. The owners of the Wanderer were tried for bringing slaves to Georgia in 1858, fifty years after slave importation became unconstitutional. The Old Cotton Exchange (1886) at 100 East Bay Street houses Solomon's Lodge, the third oldest Masonic lodge in the United States.

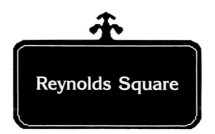

Reynolds Square

Reynolds Square (1734) is now named for the first Royal Governor of Georgia, but originally it was named Lower New Square. On August 10, 1776, the Declaration of Independence was first read to Georgians inside the colonial Council House beside this square. Until it was destroyed by fire in 1758, Savannah produced high quality silk in the Filature, a wooden warehouse also beside this square. The statue in the center of this square (pictured) honors the Reverend John Wesley, the "founder" of Methodism and one of the first rectors of Savannah's Christ Church. According to Savannah

legend, Wesley quickly lost popularity with the colonists because he regularly walked around Savannah, wrote down the "sins" that he saw other colonists commit, and then recounted those sins before his congregation!

Near this square: The Habersham-Pink House (1789) at 23 Abercorn Street survived the great Savannah fire of 1796 and, today, it houses a fine restaurant and bar.

Wright Square

Wright Square (1733) is now named for James Wright, the last Royal Governor of Georgia. It was originally named Percival Square for Georgia Trust President Lord Percival. Savannahians have often just called it "Court House Square" or "Post Office Square" though, because a courthouse (now serving as a post office) has stood beside this square since Oglethorpe's day. In 1883, Savannah erected the Gordon monument (pictured) in the center of this square to honor Savannahian William W. Gordon, who built the Central of Georgia Railroad into what was once the longest one company-railroad in the world. A

Georgia granite rock in the southeastern corner of this square honors Tomochichi, the Yamacraw Indian Chief who befriended Oglethorpe and the colonists. This rock replaced Savannah's first monument, a ballast-stone pyramid that the colonists built in the center of this square to honor Tomochichi.

Near this square: The Juliette Gordon Low Girl Scout National Center (1818) at 142 Bull Street was the birthplace of Juliette Gordon Low, the founder of the Girl Scouts of America.

Franklin Square

Franklin Square (1790) is named for Benjamin Franklin, one of America's founding fathers and Georgia's personal agent in London from 1768 to 1775. Franklin was an early benefactor of George Whitefield's Bethesda Orphanage and the friend who sent Noble Jones Chinese rice and tallow tree seeds as test crops for Wormsloe Plantation. The City of Savannah water tower stood for many years at its center, so this square has traditionally been known as "Water Tank Square," "Water Tower Square," and "Reservoir Square." In the early 1980s, this square and much of the surrounding Franklin Ward were largely renovated.

Near this square: The City Market on West St. Julian Street houses numerous restaurants, artist galleries, and handcraft shops in very old but recently renovated warehouses. The First African Baptist Church (1859) at 23 Montgomery Street and the First Bryan Baptist Church (1788) at 575 West Bryan Street house the oldest black Christian congregations in the United States.

Warren Square

Warren Square (1790) is named for Continental Army General Joseph Warren, the American Revolutionary War hero who served as President of the Third Provincial Congress of Massachusetts and died during the Battle of Bunker Hill. In the 1960s, as part of the St. Julian Street Project, the Historic Savannah Foundation restored and moved many of the houses originally in the ward surrounding this square to St. Julian and other streets.

Near this square: The John David Mongin House (1793) at 24 Habersham Street served as a hospital during the 1876 yellow fever epidemic. The Spencer House (1790) at 22 Habersham Street survived the fire of 1796 and was later renovated by the Historic Savannah Foundation.

Washington Square

Washington Square (1790) is named for George Washington, the first American President. On August 10, 1776, after first hearing the Declaration of Independence in Reynolds Square, Savannahians celebrated their first Independence Day on the land that became this square. Since modern Independence Day celebrations usually involve fireworks, it is somewhat ironic that this square long hosted a firehouse and was known as "Firehouse Square." Even more ironic though is the fact that through the early-1900s, Savannahians built building-sized bonfires in this square each New Year's eve. The ward surrounding this square was extensively renovated in the 1960s.

Near this square: The Hampton Lillibridge House (1796) at 507 East St. Julian Street was moved from 310 East Bryan Street by Jim Williams. According to legend, strange noises and disembodied voices prompted workers to stop renovating the house until Williams had an Episcopal bishop perform an exorcism on it in 1963. The International Seaman's House (1843) at 25 Houston Street is operated by the Savannah Port Society for the benefit of visiting seaman.

Columbia Square

Columbia Square (1799), like the District of Columbia, is named for Columbia, the female personage of American freedoms and namesake of Christopher Columbus. In 1971, a descendant of colonist Noble Jones restored and placed a fountain from Wormsloe Plantation in the center of this square (pictured).

Near this square: The Isaiah Davenport House (1815-21) at 324 East State Street was the first house saved by the seven ladies who eventually formed the Historic Savannah Foundation. The Kehoe House (1893, pic-

tured) at 123 Habersham Street is a hotel with a predominantly brick façade—but everything painted white is actually made of cast iron! The Bonticue House (1850) at 418 East State Street has an unusual "eyebrow" window. Laura's Cottage (1799-1808) at 420 East State Street was actually moved from Greene Square by the Historic Savannah Foundation.

Greene Square

Greene Square (1799) is named for American Revolutionary General Nathanael Greene, the Rhode Islander whose heroics earned him the title "Savior of the South." As a reward for his heroics, the State of Georgia gave Greene title to the Mulberry Grove Plantation near Savannah. Greene died soon after moving to the plantation, but his wife stayed and raised their children there. In 1793, while tutoring Greene's children, Eli Whitney invented the cotton gin on that plantation.

Near this square: The Second African Baptist Church (1925) at 123 Houston Street now stands where an 1802 church once stood. The Meyerhoff House (1840) at 521 York Street is made of what is today relatively rare Savannah gray brick from the Hermitage Plantation.

Liberty Square

Liberty Square (1799) honors the very spirit of Liberty and its embodiment in the "Sons of Liberty," an American Revolutionary group that was extremely strong in Savannah. Shortly before the American Revolution started, Savannah Sons of Liberty raided local British ammunition stores and shipped the "liberated" munitions to the Revolutionaries near Boston. The people of Boston never forgot this favor. At the end of the American Civil War, Savannah was unable to support itself by shipping Southern cotton and the citizens nearly starved to death. Luckily, the kind people of Boston remembered the actions of the Sons of Liberty and shipped boatloads of food and supplies to save the people of Savannah.

In 1985, the American Legion moved its Flame of Freedom monument from Elbert Square to this square, where it now rather ironically stands outside the Chatham County Courthouse and Jail (1978).

Near this square: St. Andrew's Independent Episcopal Church (1909, pictured) at 112 Montgomery Street was originally built as the B'nai B'rith Jacob Synagogue.

Elbert Square

Elbert Square (1801) is named for Samuel Elbert, a local farmer who was also a member of Savannah's Council of Safety, a member of the Provincial Congress of 1775, a Revolutionary War soldier, the Sheriff of Chatham County twice, and the Governor of Georgia. After the Great Fire of 1820, building plots were sold in the ward around this square and the proceeds were used to install water cisterns in each Savannah square. In the 1930s, US 17 was built through the middle of this square and Liberty Square. Each square was reduced to a strip of land a mere fraction of its original size. From 1969 to 1985, the American Legion's Flame of Freedom monument stood on this square.

Near this square: The Civic Center (1984) at 301 West Oglethorpe Avenue is the only building in Savannah that touches both the northern and southern boundaries of its ward.

Chippewa Square

Chippewa Square (1815) honors Major General Jacob Jennings Brown's victory at the Battle of Chippewa (Canada) during the War of 1812. In the center of this square, a statue of Georgia founder General James Oglethorpe (pictured) stands facing Spanish Florida with his sword unsheathed—but pointed downward. Daniel Chester French and Henry Bacon designed this statue in 1910 and then later designed the Lincoln Memorial in Washington, D.C. On the base of this statue are shields showing Oglethorpe's coat of arms and the seals of the Colony of Georgia, the State of Georgia, and the City of Savannah. A park bench was created and placed on the eastern side of this square in order to film the park bench scenes in the movie *Forrest Gump*.

Near this square: Independent Presbyterian Church (1817) at 25 West Oglethorpe Avenue has the cast-iron steeple visible in the "falling feather" scenes of the movie *Forrest Gump*. The Savannah Theater (1948) at 222 Bull Street occupies the site where noted American architect William Jay's theater once stood (1818).

Orleans Square

Orleans Square (1815) commemorates Andrew Jackson's victory at the Battle of New Orleans during the War of 1812. Jackson later became even more popular for defeating and expelling the Creek Indians from Georgia between 1829 and 1837. On October 6, 1988, Savannah celebrated its first German-American Day and broke ground on the German Memorial Fountain (pictured) in the center of the square. Exactly one year later, the German Heritage, German Friendly, and Georgia Salzburger Societies officially dedicated the magnificent reflecting fountain.

Near this square: The Champion-McAlpin-Fowlkes House (1844) at 230 Barnard Street is owned by the Society of Cincinnati for the State of Georgia. The Civic Center (1984) at 301 West Oglethorpe Avenue is the only building in Savannah that reaches both the northern and southern boundaries of its ward.

Lafayette Square

Lafayette Square (1837) is named for the Marquis de Lafayette, the Frenchman who served as Washington's Aide de Camp during the American Revolution and who later dedicated the Greene Obelisk in Johnson Square. Until 1846, the Savannah City Jail was located beside this square. In 1983, the National Society of the Colonial Dames of America installed a fountain (pictured) commemorating the 250th anniversary of the founding of the Georgia colony in the center of this square.

Near this square: The Andrew Low House (1849, pictured) at 329 Abercorn Street was built for Andrew Low. His daughter-in-law, Juliette Gordon Low, founded the Girl Scouts of America and gave them the carriage house behind this house as their first headquarters. This house now headquarters the Georgia Society of the Colonial Dames of America (1893). The Cathedral of St. John the Baptist (1876, pictured) at Abercorn and East Harris Streets is the starting point for the St. Patrick's Day parade, the key event in Savannah's annual "Mardi Gras"-styled St. Patrick's Day festivities.

Madison Square

Madison Square (1837) is named for James Madison, the fourth American President. Seldom are enlisted soldiers honored with statues, but in the center of this square stands a statue of Sergeant William Jasper (pictured), a three-time Revolutionary War hero. Because he was illiterate, Jasper declined the officer's commission that he was offered after rescuing his fallen regimental flag at the Battle of Fort Moultrie in 1776. Later that year, Jasper and John Newton rescued twelve American prisoners from the British at what became Jasper Springs, South Carolina. On October 9, 1779, Jasper died from wounds that he received while, once again, rescuing his fallen regimental flag during the Siege of Savannah. On the southern side of the square, two canons commemorate the colonial highways to Darien, Georgia and Augusta, Georgia.

Near this square: The Greene-Meldrim House (1857) at 14 West Macon Street served as Sherman's headquarters when he occupied Savannah after his "March to the Sea." After meeting with Secretary of War Stanton and representatives of freed slaves in this house, Sherman issued his Field Order #15 granting many freed slaves "Forty acres and a mule." Until the twentieth century, this house was the most expensive ever built in Savannah.

Pulaski Square

Pulaski Square (1837) is named for Count Casimir Pulaski, the highest-ranking foreign officer to die in the American Revolution. Pulaski won many revolutionary battles against the Russians in his native Poland, but was eventually forced to live in exile. Benjamin Franklin met Pulaski in Paris and recruited him to fight for the American revolutionaries. On October 9, 1779, Pulaski died during the Siege of Savannah. Savannah honored Pulaski with both a monument in Monterey Square and his own square. Georgia, as a whole, also named Fort Pulaski, Pulaski County, and the city of Pulaski after him. In the 1960s, the Historic Savannah Foundation renovated many of the homes in the ward surrounding this square.

Near this square: The Francis Bartow House (1839) at 116 West Harris Street belonged to the Confederate hero from Savannah who died during first Battle of Bull Run. The Jewish Education Alliance Building (1915) at 328 Barnard Street is now a redbrick dormitory for the Savannah College of Art and Design (SCAD).

Crawford Square

Crawford Square (1841) is named for William Harris Crawford, a Savannahian who was the Governor of Georgia, an American foreign minister to Napoleon, and Secretary of the U.S. Treasury. When Crawford ran for president in 1824, he placed third in electoral votes. When the House of Representatives eventually decided the election, they arguably failed to vote for Crawford because he had recently suffered from a debilitating illness. Although it was completely renovated with a basketball court and playground park in 1979, this square harkens back to yesteryear. First, near the gazebo in the center of this square, a cistern cover reminds visitors that—after the Great Fire of 1820—water cisterns were installed under every Savannah square. Second, this square alone has a cast iron fence (pictured) around it—but, at one time, every Savannah square was similarly fenced. Finally, there is a lot of tabby pavement (pictured) around this square. Tabby was a favorite Colonial building material, made from sea shells, lime, and water.

Near this square: Habersham Hall (1887), a building owned by the Savannah College of Art and Design (SCAD) at 235-239 Habersham Street, looks like a mosque but was originally the Chatham County Jail.

44

Chatham Square

Chatham Square (1847), like Savannah's own Chatham County, is named for William Pitt, the Earl of Chatham and the Prime Minister who wanted Parliament to treat all British citizens—including the colonists—as equals under the English Bill of Rights. During the cotton export boom that made Savannah rich in the early 1800s, many wealthy Savannahians built beautiful Greek Revival homes beside this square and throughout its ward. Each spring soft and beautiful azalea blossoms (pictured) bejewel this and almost every other Savannah square.

Near this square: The Gordon Row (1853) at 101-129 West Gordon Street is one full city block of beautifully restored three-story row houses with intricate and decorative cast iron railings. The Barnard Street School (1901) at 212 West Taylor Street was recently renovated by the Savannah College of Art and Design.

Calhoun Square

Calhoun Square (1851) is named for John C. Calhoun, the South Carolinian who was U.S. Vice-President, Secretary of State, Secretary of War, and who was known during his life as "the Great Orator of the South." In 1819, Calhoun and President James Monroe attended ceremonies in Johnson Square before ceremonially launching the historic U.S.S. Savannah steamship. During the cotton export boom that made Savannah rich in the early 1800s, many wealthy Savannahians built beautiful homes beside this square and throughout its ward.

Near this square: The Wesley Monumental United Methodist Church (1876) at 433 Abercorn Street honors Reverend John Wesley, the founder of Methodism, and his brother, Reverend Charles Wesley, who wrote "Hark! The Herald Angels Sing." The Massie Heritage Center (1856) at 201-213 East Gordon Street was built with funds from the estate of Peter Massie, a Brunswick farmer, as a school for Savannah's poor children.

Monterey Square (1851) commemorates Zachary Taylor's 1846 victory—with the help of numerous Savannah "Irish Jasper Greens" militiamen—at the Battle of Monterey (Mexico). In the center of this square, the Pulaski Monument honors Count Casimir Pulaski (see also Pulaski Square). The inverted canons and the laurel wreaths on the cast iron fence surrounding this monument symbolize military loss, victory and peace. In 1854, Pulaski's supposed remains were exhumed from Greenwich Plantation and re-interred under the monument in this square. Except for the United Way building, all of the buildings beside the square are 1850s-era originals.

Near this square: Mercer House (1871, pictured) at 429 Bull Street was built by the grandfather of famed Savannahian songwriter Johnny Mercer,

but no Mercer ever lived here. A century later, Jim Williams, the main character in *Midnight in the Garden of Good and Evil*, completely renovated this house and lived in it until his death in 1990. It is certainly Savannah's most famous, and arguably most beautiful, house. The Congregation Mickve Israel Synagogue (1878, pictured) at 20 East Gordon Street houses the third oldest Jewish congregation in America (1733).

Troup Square

Troup Square (1851) is named for George Michael Troup, a Chatham County native who served as a Congressman, a Senator, and the Governor of Georgia. Only Troup and George Washington (Washington Square and Ward) had their wards and squares named after them while they were still alive. This square is smaller than most others and made even more unique by its 1970s-era Victorian armillary (pictured) modeling the heavens and, like a sundial, revealing the time of day. This square is commonly called "Dog Bone Square" because it has a pet-friendly fountain similar to the Myers Drinking Fountain in Forsyth Park.

Near this square: The Unitarian Universalist Church (1851, pictured) at 321 Habersham Street was originally built beside Oglethorpe Square. Legend says that James Pierpont (an uncle of financier J. Pierpont Morgan) wrote the Christmas song "Jingle Bells" while serving as organist and choir director of this church. After the Civil War, freed slaves bought the building, moved it to Troup Square, and renamed it St. Stephen Episcopal Church. Today, Unitarians have reclaimed the church.

Whitefield Square

Whitefield Square (1851) is named for the Reverend George Whitefield, the fourth minister of the Georgia colony, the second rector of Christ Episcopal Church, and the founder of the Bethesda Orphanage (1740). The ward around this square is primarily filled with wooden Victorian houses. In the center of this square is a plain but beautiful gazebo (pictured) occasionally used for weddings.

Near this square: The First Congregational Church (1895) at 421 Habersham Street was built atop its predecessor (1869) for New England

Congregationalists who taught freed slaves at Savannah's Beach Institute. German architect Henry Urban designed the Beth Eden Baptist Church (1893) at 302 East Gordon Street, and also supervised the reconstruction of Independent Presbyterian Church (1899) at 25 West Oglethorpe Avenue.

Wormsloe Plantation

Wormsloe Plantation (1736) was originally named "Wormslow" by Noble Jones, the colonist who came to Savannah on Oglethorpe's first voyage and built his plantation to produce cattle, cotton, rice, and silk. A Jones-descendant later changed this plantation's name to "Wormsloe," planted 400 live oaks along its one and one-half mile driveway (in the 1890s) and erected the imposing gate at its entrance (pictured) to commemorate Noble Jones' arrival in Savannah in 1733. Unfortunately, the original tabby plantation house was not as durable as the gates, and only its ruins (pictured) now remain. In 1972, Jones' descendants donated 822 acres of the plantation to the State of Georgia (through the Nature Conservancy) for use as a public park.

Forsyth Park

Forsyth Park (1851) is named for Georgia Governor and US Secretary of State John Forsyth. William Hodgson, husband to Margaret Telfair, gave most of the land in this park to the City of Savannah. The Ladies Memorial Association erected a Confederate Monument (1875) in the park and gave it to the City of Savannah so long as its surrounding cast iron fence remains. The Confederate soldier atop this monument faces and defends against the North while the busts of Confederate heroes Bartow and McLaws guard its base. In 1858, the majestic Forsyth Fountain (pictured) was installed on the northern

side of this park. In 1897, the Myers Drinking Fountain was installed in this park to provide human water faucets and animal water bowls.

Near this park: Hodgson Hall (1875) at 501 Whitaker Street was built by Mary and Margaret Telfair in honor of Margaret's husband, William Hodgson, but solely for use by The Georgia Historic Society.

Colonial Park Cemetery

Colonial Park (1896) was originally used as Christ Church Burying Ground and as Old Colonial Cemetery (1750). Among the notables buried in this park—who also have a Georgia county named for them—are: Archibald Bulloch, the first President of Georgia; James Habersham, the Royal Governor of the Georgia Colony; Joseph Habersham, three-time American Postmaster General; Major General Lachlan McIntosh, a Revolutionary War hero; Samuel Elbert (see Elbert Square); Colonel John S. McIntosh, a hero of the War with Mexico; and Button Gwinnett, a signer of the Declaration of Independence.

Mass graves were dug during at least one yellow fever epidemic and encamped Union soldiers misplaced and destroyed many headstones, so most gravesites are approximate. When community service organizations restored this park, they placed the "misplaced" headstones against the rear brick wall of this park (pictured). American Revolutionary War hero Nathanael Greene was also buried in this park, until he was exhumed and re-interred under the obelisk in Johnson Square in 1901.

Bonaventure Cemetery

Bonaventure Cemetery (1907) is a beautiful remnant of the Bonaventure Plantation that South Carolinian John Mullryne began amassing in 1753. During the American Revolution, some French soldiers may have been buried there since the plantation house served as a French hospital. However, the first recorded burial at Bonaventure Plantation was much later. Harriet Fenwick Tattnall, the wife of Mullryne's youngest grandson, was the first person officially buried at Bonaventure in 1802. The Evergreene Cemetery Company of Bonaventure was not formally incorporated as a public cemetery until 1847. The City of Savannah

bought and renamed it Bonaventure Cemetery in 1907. Academy-Award winning songwriter Johnny Mercer and Pulitzer Prize winning poet Conrad Aiken are among the many noted Savannahians buried in this cemetery. Mercer's grave is near the angel pictured above. The Bird Girl statue made famous by the book and movie *Midnight in the Garden of Good and Evil* was originally in this cemetery, but it was moved to the Telfair Museum of Art (see Telfair Square) in 1997. A statue of Savannah's legendary "Gracie" Watson sits atop her grave.

Chatham Area Transit Historic District Shuttle Map

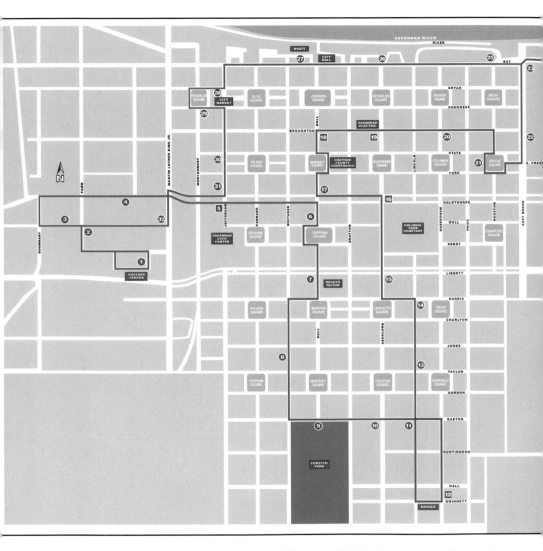

Map courtesy of Chatham Area Transit (CAT). For more information, visit www.catchacat.org or call 912-233-5767.